WOMEN
Who Changed History

Adam Sutherland

WAYLAND

Published in 2014 by Wayland

Wayland
338 Euston Road
London NW1 3BH

Wayland Australia
Hachette Children's Books
Level 17/207
Kent Street
Sydney, NSW 2000

First published in 2013 by Wayland

Editor: Nicola Edwards
Designer: Tim Mayer, MayerMedia

A CIP catalogue record for this book is available from the British Library.
ISBN 978 0 7502 8390 8

Wayland is a division of Hachette Children's Books, as Hachette UK company
www.hachette.co.uk

Picture acknowledgements
Cover: David Simon/Gamma-Rapho via Getty Images; title page: Getty Images; p2 Khin Maung Win/AP/Press Association Images; p5 (b) Getty Images; p9 Getty Images; p10 Nobel Foundation; p11 Time & Life Pictures/ Getty Images; p12 Gamma-Rapho via Getty Images; p13 STF/AFP/Getty Images; p14 Tim Graham/Getty Images; p15 Getty Images; p16 Neftall/Shutterstock. com; p17 Khin Maung Win/AP/Press Association Images; p18 GIANLUIGI GUERCIA/AFP/Getty Images; p19 Junko Kimura/Getty Images; p20 catwalker/Shutterstock.com; p21 Getty Images; p22 (bl) Getty Images, (tm) Sylvana Rega/Shutterstock.com, (bm) paulinux / Shutterstock. com; (br) Rudolf Simon

The website addresses (URLs) and QR codes included in this book were valid at the time of going to press. However it is possible that contents and addresses may have changed since the publication of this book. No responsibility for any such changes can be accepted by either the author or the Publisher.

CONTENTS

Words in **bold** can be found in the glossary on page 24.

Making History

In Britain, women under 21 could not vote until 1928. The United States had only allowed women the vote eight years earlier. Historically, women have been banned from certain professions and today, in certain parts of the world, girls are still being excluded from education, and women not being granted the same legal rights as men.

The history makers in this book have all refused to accept the rules that their countries or societies had set for them. These women would not take no for an answer. How many of us, faced with the challenges of Elizabeth Garrett Anderson (page 8) would have kept on fighting for equality? Determined to be a doctor, she saw all her applications for medical school rejected. When she persevered and privately passed her exams, no hospital in the country would hire her, so she started her own!

Elizabeth Garrett Anderson (left) and Emmeline Pankhurst: both campaigners advanced the rights of women in Victorian Britain.

Visitors pass in front of the Marie Curie memorial in the scientist's native Poland.

Bravery is a huge part of becoming a history maker. The bravery of Rosa Parks (page 16) who refused to give up her seat on a bus for a white passenger and sparked huge advances in the civil rights movements. The courage of Wangari Maathai (page 18) who stood up against her own government, and fought for conservation and advances in female employment. Or the bravery of Pakistani schoolgirl Malala Yousafzai (page 21) who risked death to speak out against the Taliban's ban on girls' education. Yousafzai survived an **assassination** attempt and continues to campaign today. Read on and prepare to be inspired.

Suffagette Emmeline Pankhurst (page 9) even encouraged her supporters to use violence if necessary, to achieve their aims of equal votes for women. She was fortunate enough to achieve her lifetime's ambition just before her death.

Coco Chanel (page 12) and Marie Curie (page 10), although very different women, both entered professions that had previously been exclusively reserved for men, and made incredible breakthroughs – in design and research. The fashion and science worlds would be poorer without their efforts.

Civil rights protester Rosa Parks riding a bus in Montgomery, Alabama, in 1956.

Mary Seacole
Unsung heroine

The daughter of a Scottish soldier and a Jamaican Creole 'doctress', Seacole learned traditional Caribbean and African herbal medicine from her mother and practised her skills on the guests at the family hotel in Kingston, Jamaica.

Crimean War

During a visit to Britain in 1853, Seacole learned about the **Crimean War** and how the nursing system was nearing collapse, with many wounded soldiers dying of **cholera**. She was refused permission through the War Office to lend her services, but eventually made her own way to the front in 1855.

This photograph of Mary Seacole was taken in 1873.

Name: Mary Jane Grant (married Edwin Seacole in 1836)

Born: 1805 in Kingston, Jamaica (exact date unknown)

Died: 14 May 1881 in London, England

Achievements: Awarded the Jamaican Order of Merit (1991), first place in a poll of 100 Great Black Britons (2004), image used on a series of UK postage stamps in 2005 portraying important Britons.

Interesting fact: Seacole's life story was introduced into the National Curriculum in 2007, alongside Florence Nightingale.

> **❝** I trust that England will not forget one who nursed her sick, who sought out her wounded to aid... them. **❞**
>
> *WH Russell*

Helping the sick

Seacole established her own 'British Hotel' behind enemy lines – caring for the sick, and attending to the wounded on the battlefield. She had bought all her own supplies, and the end of the war left her financially **bankrupt**. Back in Britain, her efforts were largely **overlooked** for many years, although more recently she has been widely recognized and praised for her bravery and good work.

Florence Nightingale
Lady with the lamp

Nightingale was born into a wealthy upper-class family but early in life she rejected the expected route of marriage and children, and decided to dedicate herself to nursing. She was fortunate to have a very forward-thinking father who taught her Greek, Latin, history, philosophy and mathematics. Nevertheless, it took six years of pressure before Nightingale received his permission to start nursing training.

Fighting infection

Nightingale travelled to the Crimean War in 1854 with 38 nurses she had personally trained. Once there, she found that dirty conditions and a severe lack of medical supplies meant that ten times more soldiers were dying of infections than from battle wounds. Her plea to *The Times* newspaper persuaded the government to increase funding, reducing the death rate by 90 per cent.

Equal healthcare

Nightingale's efforts caught the British public's imagination. The Nightingale Fund was established to provide training for nurses, and by 1860 she had £45,000 to set up the Nightingale Training School at St Thomas' Hospital – the first of its kind in the world. She also trained American Linda Richards, who returned home to establish nursing schools across the USA.

Name: Florence Nightingale

Born: 12 May 1820 in Florence, Italy

Died: 13 August 1910 in London, England

Achievements: The Nightingale Pledge, taken by all new nurses, is named in her honour. International Nurses Day takes place annually on her birthday.

Interesting fact: Both Florence and her sister Parthenope Nightingale were named after the cities where they were born. Parthenopolis was a Greek settlement in the Italian city of Naples.

Florence Nightingale's efforts brought about improved healthcare in Britain and showed that women had a valuable role to play in the workplace.

Elizabeth Garrett Anderson
Medical pioneer

Name: Elizabeth Garrett Anderson

Born: 9 June 1836 in Whitechapel, London, UK

Died: 17 December 1917 in Aldeburgh, Suffolk, UK

Achievements: First Englishwoman to qualify as a doctor and a surgeon in Britain, co-founder of the first hospital staffed by women, first dean of a British medical school, first female MD in France.

Interesting fact: In retirement, she was the first female mayor in England.

to attend lectures for male doctors, until complaints from fellow students led to her being banned. She continued to study privately, and passed her medical exams at the top of her class.

Elizabeth Garrett Anderson's life was full of dedication, hard work, and a refusal to take no for an answer. Meetings with **feminist** Emily Davies, and American **physician** Elizabeth Blackwell made her determined to become a doctor.

Persevering

Anderson was undeterred when all her applications to medical school were rejected. She enrolled as a nursing student, and started

Helping others

As a woman doctor, no hospital would employ her, so Anderson opened her own – the New Hospital for Women. In the first year, she treated 3,000 new patients. Her reputation finally began to break down **prejudices**, and in 1870 she was named one of the visiting physicians at the East London Hospital for Children. In 1874, she co-founded the London School of Medicine for Women, which later became part of University College London's medical school.

Emmeline Pankhurst

Fighting for women's rights

Pankhurst was born into a politically active family, and was introduced to the women's suffrage movement (the call for equal voting rights for women) through her mother. In 1879, she married Richard Pankhurst, a fellow supporter of women's rights, and her own interest **crystalized** into action.

Fighting for equal rights

In 1889 Pankhurst founded the Women's Franchise League, which campaigned to allow married women the vote. In 1903 she helped form the more **militant** Women's Social and Political Union (WPSU), which focused on 'deeds not words'. The group made headlines when members smashed windows and assaulted police officers, and Pankhurst and fellow supporters were often arrested (see photo top right of page) and put in prison.

War-time victory

At the outbreak of World War I, Pankhurst called for supporters to end campaigning and support the war effort – encouraging men to fight, and women to work to support the troops. In 1918, the Representation of the People Act gave voting rights to women over 30. In 1928, shortly before Pankhurst's death, women were finally given equal voting rights to men.

> 66 [Emmeline Pankhurst was] the most remarkable political and social agitator of the early… twentieth century. 99

New York Herald Tribune

Name: Emmeline Goulden

Born: 15 July 1858 in Moss Side, Manchester, UK

Died: 14 June 1928 in Hampstead, London, UK

Achievements: Named one of the 100 Most Important People of the 20th Century by TIME magazine (1999), ranked No 27 in a BBC poll of the 100 Greatest Britons (2002).

Interesting fact: In 1987 Pankhurst's family home in Moss Side was opened as the Pankhurst Centre museum.

Marie Curie
Nobel Prize-winning scientist

Along with her husband Pierre, Marie Curie's **groundbreaking** research into radioactivity and X-rays helped make huge advances into the treatment of cancer and other illnesses. The pair also discovered two new elements, polonium and radium, and attracted much-needed funding to their field of study.

Name: Marie Salomea Sklodowska

Born: 7 November 1867 in Warsaw, Poland

Died: 4 July 1934 in Haute-Savoie, France

Achievements: Nobel Prize in Physics (1903), Nobel Prize in Chemistry (1911). Voted 'the most inspirational woman in science' by New Scientist (2009).

Interesting fact: The curie (symbol Ci), a unit of radioactivity, is named in honour of Curie and her husband.

Marie Curie pictured in 1903, the year she won the Nobel Prize with husband, Pierre.

Fighting for an education

Curie was unable to attend the men-only university in Warsaw, so she studied at the city's secret, underground 'Flying University'. Curie and her sister Bronislawa took turns working, so the other could devote herself to study. Eventually Curie saved enough money to move to Paris where she enrolled at the Sorbonne. She completed a master's degree in physics in 1893, and a degree in maths just one year later! At this time, she found her first job studying the magnetism of steel, where she met and married French physicist Pierre Curie.

Marie and Pierre Curie at work in their laboratory. Between 1898 and 1902, the couple published 32 papers on their work.

Research into radioactivity

At first, husband and wife worked on separate projects. Marie investigated uranium rays, creating the new field of atomic physics and even inventing a new word 'radioactivity' to describe her work. Soon Pierre put aside his own research to work alongside his wife. In 1898 the pair discovered a new radioactive element, which they named polonium after her native Poland. By 1902, they had also discovered radium, and a year later they shared the Nobel Prize for their work on radioactivity.

Working alone

In 1906, Pierre was killed in a road accident, but Curie kept on working. She became the Sorbonne's first female professor, and in 1911 won her second Nobel Prize. By the start of World War I, she had developed portable X-ray machines for the battlefield, and through regular fundraising visits to the US, managed to establish her radium research institute in Warsaw. Curie's proximity to such dangerous substances finally took their toll and she died in 1934, through prolonged exposure to radiation.

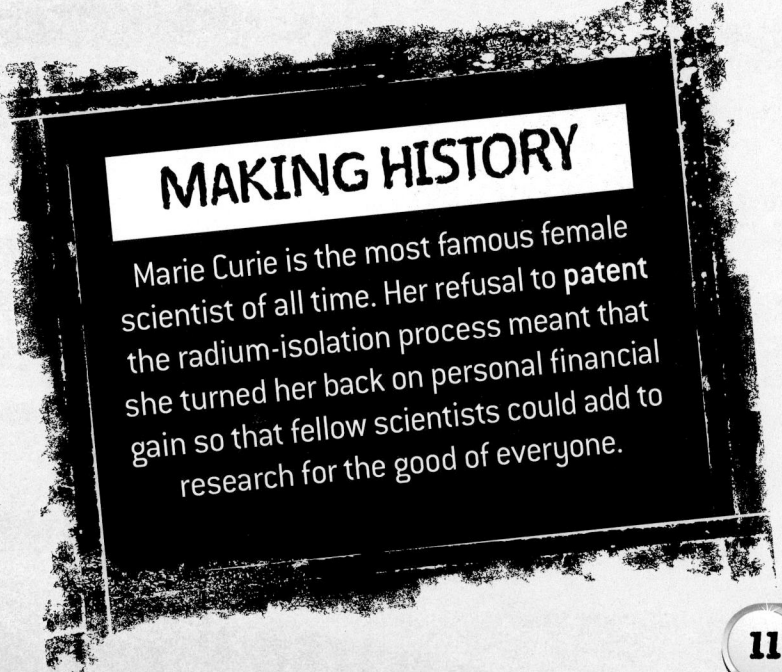

MAKING HISTORY

Marie Curie is the most famous female scientist of all time. Her refusal to **patent** the radium-isolation process meant that she turned her back on personal financial gain so that fellow scientists could add to research for the good of everyone.

Coco Chanel
Inspirational designer

Coco Chanel raised herself from a penniless orphan to become one of the world's most successful fashion designers through her modern, **liberating** womenswear designs, and her own determination and valuable social connections. Her little black dresses, and simple well-cut suits freed women from the restrictions of corsets and made Chanel a household name.

Hard times

When Chanel's mother died of bronchitis in 1895, her father sent 12-year-old Chanel and her two sisters to an orphanage in Corrèze, central France. It was here that Chanel learned to sew, and when she left at 18 she found work as a **seamstress**. In the evenings, she sang in local cabarets to earn extra money. By 1910 Chanel had begun designing hats, and opened a boutique in Paris selling her own designs.

Coco Chanel in her apartment on Rue Cambon in Paris, in 1954. The designer opened her first boutique on the street in 1919.

> **“** Luxury must be comfortable, otherwise it is not luxury. **”**
>
> *Coco Chanel*

Name: Gabrielle Bonheur Chanel

Born: 19 August 1883 in Saumur, France

Died: 10 January 1971 in Paris, France

Achievements: The only fashion designer to appear on TIME magazine's list of the 100 Most Influential People of the 20th Century.

Interesting fact: Her nickname Coco came from Chanel's time as a nightclub singer, and is thought to come from a song she used to perform.

Finding success

It was around this time that Chanel met and fell in love with Arthur Edward Capel, a wealthy English gentleman. Capel financed her first clothes boutique, which opened in Deauville in 1913, selling deluxe casual clothing, often made from flexible, comfortable fabrics such as jersey. She often told a story that she once made a dress for herself out of some old jersey, and was asked by so many people where she bought it, that she decided to make it professionally.

Building the Chanel brand

In the 1920s, Chanel introduced her now famous 'little black dress', and the perfume, Chanel No 5 – the first fragrance to carry a designer's name. In 1931, she travelled to California to design costumes for Hollywood stars Greta Garbo and Marlene Dietrich among others.

Back in France, she designed for a number of French films, as well as for the *Ballets Russes* and for playwright Jean Cocteau.

Controversy

At the start of World War II, Chanel shut down her business, putting 3,000 seamstresses out of work. She made her home at the Ritz, and was widely criticized for having an affair with a high-ranking German officer, Hans Gunther von Dincklage. After the war, she was questioned as a **collaborator**, and although never charged, her reputation in France never fully recovered. Nevertheless, her creations changed the fashion world forever.

Chanel celebrates the opening of the spring-summer collection in Paris, in 1958 accompanied by ballet dancer, Jacques Chazot.

Mother Teresa
Helping the world's poor

Young Teresa

Teresa's father died when she was just eight, and she was strongly influenced by her religious and charitable mother who often opened her home to feed the city's poor and hungry. At 18, she left home and joined the Loreto Sisters of Dublin, taking the name Sister Mary Teresa. She became a teacher at Saint Mary's High School for Girls in Calcutta, teaching girls from the city's poorest areas. By 1944 she was the school's head.

Mother Teresa took her name from the patron saint of missionaries, Thérèse de Lisieux.

Mother Teresa's life was spent helping others. At 18 years old she joined the Sisters of Loreto as a **missionary**, travelling first to Ireland to learn English and then a year later on to India to begin her training. By the time of her death, nearly 70 years later, she led an organization of over 4,000 sisters, operating 600 missions in 120 countries.

Name: Anjezë Gonxhe Bojaxhiu

Born: 26 August 1910 in Skopje, Macedonia

Died: 5 September 1997 in Calcutta, India

Achievements: Awarded the Nobel Peace Prize (1979), ranked first in a US poll of Most Widely Admired People of the 20th Century (1999).

Interesting fact: Indian Railways named a new train, the Mother Express, in 2010 to mark the centenary of her birth.

A new calling

In 1946, Mother Teresa experienced what she believed was a message from God, who told her to abandon teaching in order to work in the slums of Calcutta with the city's poor and sick. She was eventually given permission to leave her work at Saint Mary's High School and after six months' basic medical training, she travelled into the slums with no means of supporting herself and no knowledge of what she would experience.

Helping the sick and in need

At first, Mother Teresa had to beg for money to even feed herself. She eventually found her feet, however, and by 1950 she had founded the Missionaries of Charity with 12 former teachers and pupils from her old school. Donations started to pour in, not just from India but from around the world. Over the next 50 years, Mother Teresa founded countless orphanages, nursing homes, mobile health clinics and leper colonies in India, South America, Africa and Eastern Europe, and was a familiar and encouraging presence in time of tragedy and crisis. When she died, Mother Teresa was granted a state funeral in India, and was mourned around the world.

MAKING HISTORY

Mother Teresa's faith, as well as exceptional organizational skills allowed her to build a huge international network of missionaries to help poor and suffering citizens worldwide.

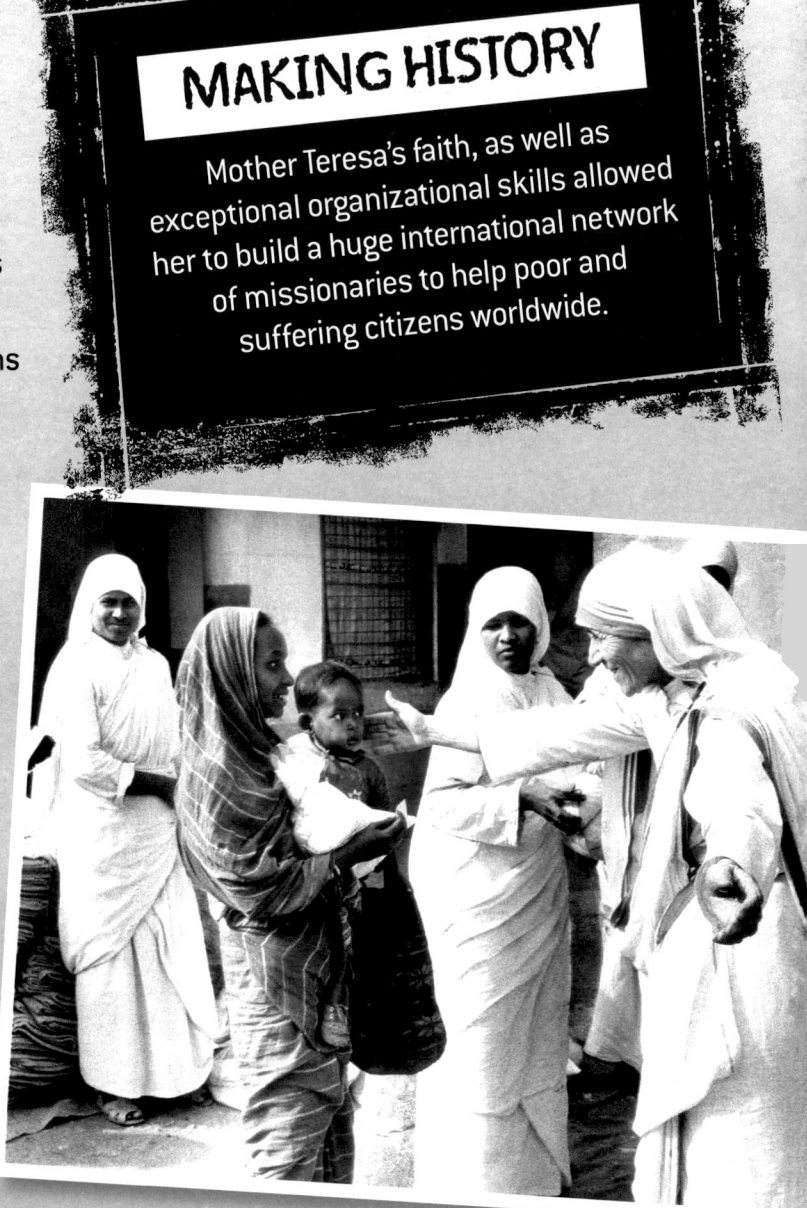

Mother Teresa (far right), accompanied by some of her Sisters of Charity, working with lepers in Calcutta, India, in 1971.

> **"** Her lifelong devotion to the poor, the sick, and the disadvantaged was one of the highest examples of services to our humanity. **"**
>
> *Nawaz Sharif, Prime Minister of Pakistan*

Rosa Parks
Civil rights activist

Rosa Parks

Parks grew up with her mother and grandparents – two former slaves – in rural Alabama. She attended segregated (blacks-only) schools that often lacked basic equipment like desks. Parks and her fellow pupils had to walk to school, while white pupils took the bus.

Boycott the buses

At 19, she married Raymond Parks, an active member of the NAACP (see right), and became involved in the struggle for civil rights. On 1 December 1955, Parks was riding the bus home from work when she was asked to give up her seat for a white passenger. She refused, and was arrested. Members of the African-American community, including civil rights leader Martin Luther King, launched a **boycott** of city buses that eventually lasted 381 days. Some walked 20 miles to work every day!

Name: Rose Louise McCauley

Born: 4 February 1913 in Yuskegee, Alabama, USA

Died: 24 October 2005 in Detroit, Michigan, USA

Achievements: Received the Spingarn Medal, the highest award of the NAACP (National Association for the Advancement of Coloured People), Presidential Medal of Freedom (1996), named in TIME magazine's '20 Most Influential People of the 20th Century'.

Interesting fact: The bus that Rosa Parks was riding in December 1955 is on display in the Henry Ford museum in Detroit.

Victory over segregation

In June 1956, the US court ruled that Alabama's racial segregation laws were **unconstitutional** and ordered them to be dropped. Rosa Parks' simple act of defiance set in motion a chain of events that helped change the United States for the better.

> " In a single moment, with the simplest of gestures, [Rosa Parks] helped change America and change the world. "
>
> *President Barack Obama*

Aung San Suu Kyi
Pro-democracy leader

Aung San Suu Kyi is the daughter of former Burmese leader Aung San, who was assassinated when she was only two. Suu Kyi grew up in Burma, India and the UK, and studied at Oxford University before returning to Burma in 1988.

Fight for democracy

In the same year, Burma's military government was reported to have killed up to 5,000 pro-democracy protestors. Suu Kyi wanted to help free her country from oppression so she joined a new political party, the National League for Democracy (NLD), and gave pro-democracy speeches up and down the country.

Arrest and freedom

In 1990, Suu Kyi was detained by the government and held under house arrest for five years. By 2000, she was arrested again after several attempts to hold political meetings. Until her final release in 2010, Suu Kyi had spent over 15 years under house arrest. She is one of the world's most prominent political prisoners, and continues to campaign for democracy in her country.

Full name: Aung San Suu Kyi

Born: 19 June 1945 in Rangoon, British Burma

Honours and achievements: Nobel Peace Prize (1991), Sakharov Prize for Freedom of Thought (1990), Wallenberg Medal (2011), Congressional Gold Medal (2012).

Interesting fact: Suu Kyi's father secured Burma's independence from the British Empire.

Aung San Suu Kyi greets supporters in 2012. She is one of the world's most prominent non-violent campaigners for democracy and human rights.

Wangari Maathai
African environmentalist

Maathai's outspoken defence of conservation areas in her homeland, and her attempts to empower women through access to work and education, often put her on a collision course with Kenya's government who called her 'a mad woman' and 'a threat to the security of the country'. Nevertheless, Maathai won worldwide support and continued to fight for what she believed in right up to her death.

Early years

Maathai was born in the highlands of Kenya, in a small village that had been home to her family for generations. At eleven, she was sent to a Catholic boarding school where she learned English and graduated at the top of her class. In 1960 she became one of 300 Kenyans selected to study in the United States through an exchange program organized by then senator John F Kennedy.

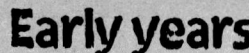

Maathai speaking at a conference in Tokyo in 2008, aiming at boosting economic growth in Africa.

Name: Wangari Muta Maathai

Born: 1 April 1940 in Nyeri District, Kenya

Died: 25 September 2011 in Nairobi, Kenya

Achievements: First African woman, and first environmentalist to win the Nobel Peace Prize (2004), first President of the African Union's Economic, Social and Cultural Council (2005)

Interesting fact: Like Maathai, President Barack Obama's father was born in Kenya and educated in America through the same exchange program.

Return to Kenya

After she received a degree in 1964, and a master's (higher) degree in 1966, Maathai returned to Kenya and began teaching at the University of Nairobi. She became the first East African woman to receive a **Ph.D.** (1971) and while there campaigned for equal rights for women on the university staff. Through voluntary work with the Red Cross and other organizations she became convinced that the root of Kenya's problems was environmental destruction.

Fighting the government

Maathai founded the Green Belt Movement and devoted the rest of her life to green issues – planting trees to conserve the environment, providing jobs and training for 30,000 women, and often directly criticizing the government on projects that would destroy the country's green areas. Although she suffered official criticism and even imprisonment at home for her views, her bravery and vision were recognized around the world. Today, the Pan-African Green Belt Network has planted over 50 million trees across Africa.

MAKING HISTORY

Wangari Maathai fought against her own government to protect the environment and support the rights of women. Her work formed an important part of the ecofeminist movement.

Maathai plants a tree in the Newlands forest, South Africa. She remained devoted to green issues throughout her life.

Anne Frank
Teenage diarist

> **"** I don't want to have lived in vain... I want to be useful or bring enjoyment to all people... I want to go on living even after my death! **"**
>
> *Anne Frank*

Jewish teenager Anne Frank is one of the best-known victims of the Nazi Holocaust. Her diaries, written while she was in hiding and published after World War II, have been translated into 60 languages.

Leaving Germany

When Frank was just four, her family left their hometown of Frankfurt to escape the **anti-Semitism** that was growing under Adolf Hitler's Nazi Party. However, their new home in Amsterdam was occupied in the early days of World War II when Germany invaded Holland.

In hiding

In July 1942, Frank's mother received an official summons to a Nazi work camp back in Germany. The whole family went into hiding, making their home in a dark, cramped space in her father's offices. In August 1944 they were discovered and sent to concentration camps where Frank and her sister Margot died of **typhus**. Returning to Amsterdam after the war, Frank's father discovered her diary, which recorded two years of the teenager's hopes, fears and wisdom. *The Diary of a Young Girl* was first published in 1947, and has remained a best-seller ever since.

Name: Annelies Marie Frank

Born: 12 June 1929 in Frankfurt am Main, Germany

Died: March 1945 in Bergen-Belsen concentration camp, Germany

Achievements: Anne Frank's Diary was voted one of the Top 10 books that defined the 20th Century by The Guardian. Named one of The Most Important People of the Century by TIME magazine (1999).

Interesting fact: Asteroid 5535 was named Annefrank in her honour.

Malala Yousafzai
Schoolgirl activist

The Pakistani schoolgirl wrote a blog for the BBC about life under the Taliban, and spoke out in favour of equal education for girls. She was shot in the head in an assassination attempt, but survived and continues her pioneering work on girls' education from her new home in the UK.

In the Swat Valley

In 2009 Taliban militants took control of the Swat Valley where Yousafzai lived. They banned television, music, and education for girls. Yousafzai, who was mostly taught by her father, Ziauddin, an educational activist, spoke out against the new restrictions. 'How dare the Taliban take away my basic right to education?' she asked local journalists.

Sentenced to death

BBC Urdu asked Yousafzai to write about her experiences. Her identity was supposed to be hidden, but the brave schoolgirl often gave speeches and attended meetings in favour of girls' education. The Taliban sent a gunman to kill Yousafzai. Despite being shot in the head, she survived and was eventually flown to Britain for recuperation, and surgery to restore her hearing. She now attends school in Birmingham and continues her fight for girls' education.

Name: Malala Yousafzai

Born: 12 July 1997 in Mingora, Pakistan

Achievements: The winner of Pakistan's first National Youth Peace Prize (2011), youngest person to be nominated for the Nobel Peace Prize, named in TIME magazine's '100 Most Influential People in the World' list (2013).

Interesting fact: Yousafzai's autobiography 'I Am Malala' was published in 2013.

" Every girl in the Swat Valley is Malala. We will educate ourselves. We will win. They can't defeat us. "

Classmate of Yousafzai

Other Women Who Changed History

Mary Wollstonecraft (1759-1797)

A writer and feminist philosopher who published *A Vindication of the Rights of Women* in 1792. In it, Wollstonecraft argued for equal rights between the sexes, saying that women were not inferior to men, but simply lacked access to education. Her work and personal life were criticized, but today she is respected for her **enlightened** views.

Marie Stopes (1880-1958)

An early campaigner for women's rights, Stopes co-founded Britain's first birth control clinic with her husband Humphrey Verdon Roe. She was against abortion, and believed in prevention of pregnancy by means of contraception. There are now over 600 Marie Stopes clinics in 40 countries, advising on family planning, and HIV/AIDS prevention.

Eleanor Roosevelt (1884-1962)

The longest-serving first lady of the United States, as the wife of Franklin D Roosevelt, president from 1933-45. She spoke at national conferences, and even publicly disagreed with her husband's policies. After his death, she was the first chairperson of the United Nations Commission on Human Rights, and led John F Kennedy's Presidential Commission on the Status of Women.

Amelia Earhart (1897-1937)

The first female pilot to fly solo across the Atlantic, Earhart was awarded the US Distinguished Flying Cross, and helped form the Ninety-Nines, an organization for female pilots. She was also a member of the National Woman's Party, and an early supporter of the Equal Rights Amendment, which was designed to guarantee equal rights for women.

Martha Gelhorn (1908-1998)

An American travel writer and journalist, Gelhorn was considered to be one of the 20th century's greatest war correspondents. In a 60-year career she reported on almost every major world conflict from the Spanish Civil War to World War II, Vietnam and the Middle East. Lifelong friends with Eleanor Roosevelt, she blazed a trail for other female writers to follow.

Angela Merkel (1954-present)

The leader of Germany's Christian Democratic Union (CDU) since 2000 and her country's Chancellor since 2005, Merkel is the first woman to hold either office. She was inspired to enter politics by the East German and Czech revolutions of 1989. Elected as an MP in 1990, she has been ranked as the second most powerful person in world politics behind Barack Obama.

Timeline

Legacy

1855 Mary Seacole travels to the Crimean War

1860 Florence Nightingale establishes the world's first nurse training school at St Thomas's Hospital

1874 Elizabeth Garrett Anderson co-founds the London School of Medicine for Women

1876 Women are finally allowed to enter the medical profession

1903 Emmeline Pankhurst forms the Women's Social and Political Union (WPSU)

1903 Marie and Pierre Curie awarded the Nobel Prize

1911 Marie Curie wins her second Nobel Prize

1913 Coco Chanel opens her first designer boutique in Deauville, France

1921 Marie Stopes co-founds Britain's first birth control clinic

1928 UK women given equal voting rights to men

1928 Amelia Earhart flies solo across the Atlantic

1947 Anne Frank's *Diary of a Young Girl* published

1950 Mother Teresa founds the Missionaries of Charity to help India's poor and sick

1955 Rosa Parks refuses to give up her seat on a bus to a white passenger

1990 Aung San Suu Kyi arrested and detained for five years

2004 Wangari Maathai awarded the Nobel Peace Prize for her 'contribution to sustainable development, democracy and peace'

2005 Angela Merkel voted Chancellor of Germany

2012 Malala Yousafzai shot in the head by a Taliban gunman

2013 Malala Yousafzai addresses a UN conference on her 16th birthday, saying that the Taliban's efforts to silence her had failed

The legacies of the women in this book live on, not only in their achievements but also through the work of their families and followers:

http://www.mariecurie.org.uk/
A UK charity set up in 1948 to provide free nursing care to terminally ill people. In 2010/11 it helped 32,000 people, and employed over 2,500 doctors, nurses and other healthcare professionals.

http://www.greenbeltmovement.org
Founded by Wangari Maathai in 1977, the Green Belt Movement empowers communities – particularly women – to conserve their environment and improve their standard of living.

http://womenone.org/news/the-malala-fund/
Malala Yousafzai's charity supports the education and empowerment of girls in Pakistan and around the world. It provides grants to organisations and individuals focused on education. Actress Angelina Jolie has already pledged US$200,000.

Glossary

Index

activist A person who believes in social or political change, and often takes part in activities, such as marches, to try to make this happen.

anti-Semitism Anti-Jewish prejudice.

assassination Killing, murder.

bankrupt Having no money; unable to pay what you owe.

boycott A refusal to buy a company's products or use its services as a form of protest.

cholera A serious stomach infection caused by drinking infected water or eating infected food. Can cause death.

collaborator In wartime, a person who cooperates with an enemy force occupying the country

Crimean War A war between the Russian Empire and an alliance of the UK, France, Sardinian and the Ottoman Empire.

crystallised formed into a strong belief or conviction.

dean A high ranking official at a college or university.

enlightened Showing understanding, acting in a positive way, not following traditional or old-fashioned beliefs.

environmentalist Someone who is interested in the environment, and who tries to protect it against damage.

feminist A person who believes that women should be allowed the same rights, powers and opportunities as men, and should be treated in the same way.

groundbreaking Completely new or different from what has gone before.

liberating Making you feel free and able to heave as you like.

MD A doctor of medicine.

militant Active, determined, and often willing to use force.

missionary A person who is sent to a foreign country to teach their religion to the people who live there.

overlooked Not to be noticed or praised for hard work, courage or achievement.

patent To be awarded the legal right to make or sell an invention for a particular number of years.

Ph.D The highest college or university degree. Stands for Doctor of Philosophy.

physician Another word for a doctor.

pioneer One of the first people to do something new.

prejudice An unfair and unreasonable opinion or feeling, formed without sufficient thought or information.

seamstress A woman whose job is sewing and making clothes.

typhus An infectious disease spread by lice (small insects that live on the body) that causes high temperature, severe pains and a rash.

unconstitutional Not allowed according to the rules or constitution of a particular country.